Songs for Discharming

Poems by
Denise Sweet

Greenfield Review Press

Publication of this book has been made possible, in part, through a grant from the Lannan Foundation.

This book was the winner of the North American Native Authors First Book Award: The Diane Decorah Award for Poetry

Songs for Discharming
Poems by Denise Sweet

ISBN 0-912678-95-X

Some of the poems in *Songs for Discharming* have previously appeared in the following publications: *Another Chicago Magazine, Akwekon, Calyx, Returning the Gift, Sinister Wisdom, Women Brave in the Face of Danger, Wisconsin Poetry,* and *Days of Obsidian, Days of Grace.*

Library of Congress Number: 97-070245

Cover Art by Scott Hill
Copyright © 1997 by Scott Hill

Design by Vivian L. Bradbury
Composition by Sans Serif, Inc.
Saline, Michigan

The Greenfield Review Press
Greenfield Center, N.Y. 12833

Distributed by The Talman Company, Inc.
131 Spring Street
New York, NY 10012

For Damon and Vaughn

In memory of Veda Stone,
Thunderbird Sky Woman

Contents

Song for Discharming   *1*

Migration   *3*

Doing Time   *5*

Still Born   *7*

The Origin of Envy   *9*

My Good Fortune   *12*

By the Sound of It   *14*

Homing Song: Two Stanzas   *17*

Found Poem or Sometimes I Hate My Job   *19*

Trickster   *20*

Constellations   *21*

To Know by Heart: Saulte St. Marie, October 1989   *22*

In September: Ode to Tomatoes   *24*

Here in America   *26*

Mission at White Earth   *28*

For Children Who Earn Time   *30*

Fever Dreams   *32*

Water Poem: A Convergence   *34*

Evelyn Searching: To My Sister   *36*

Prayer for Women Filled With Grace   *38*

My Mother and I had a Discussion One Day   *40*

Losing to the Breakfast of Champions   *42*

Winter Farm Auction   *43*

Grace's Funeral   *45*

Club Med at UxMal, Yucatan   *46*

Veteran's Dance, 1995   *48*

Insomniac   *49*

The 500-year-old Poem   *51*

Acknowledgements

I would like to recognize the support and advice extended by the following: Patrick McKinnon, Walt Bresette, Geary Hobson, Bruce Taylor, Carlos Cumpian, Joy Harjo, and Barry Silesky.

Song For Discharming

*"Hear the voice of my song— it is my voice
I speak to your naked heart."* — Chippewa Charming Song

Before this, I would not do or say what impulse
rushes in to say or do
what instinct burns within
I had learned to temper in my clever sick
while stars unlock at dawn, anonymous as the speed of light
my gray mornings began as nothing, freed of geography
and stripped of any source or consequence.
I was, as you may expect, a human parenthesis.
There is no simple way to say this,
but drift closer, Invisible One, swim within this stream
of catastrophic history. Yours? Mine?
No, you decide. And then

come here one more time so that I may numb like dark
and desperate, so that I may speak your name this final round
you might think an infinite black fog waits to envelope me
you might dream an endless flat of light
you might think I drink
at the very edge of you, cowering like passerine while
hawks hunt the open field of my tiny wars.

but, little by little, like centipedes that whirl and spin
and sink into scorching sands of Sonora
or like gulls at Moningwanekaning that rise and stir
and vanish into the heat lightning of August
I will call you down and bring you into that deathly coil
I will show you each step and stair

1

I will do nothing and yet it will come to you in this way
that sorcery that swallowed me will swallow you too
at your desired stanza and in a manner of your own making

While I shake the rattle of ferocity moments before sunrise
while I burn sage and sweetgrass, and you, my darling,
while I burn you like some ruined fetish and sing over you
over and over like an almighty voice from the skies
it is in that fragile light
that I will love you
it is in that awakening
I will love myself too
in this dry white drought about to end
in this ghostly city of remember

You will know this, too
and never be able to say.

> Moningwanekoning: (Chippewa) Madeline Island, Lake
>   Superior.
> See migration narratives of Chippewa/Anishinabeeg.

2

Migration

"The furies of nature make migration dangerous, especially for the young, the old, the ill. Animals have no choice about when to start their journeys. They must go when it is time." — Dennis Flanagan, "Beautiful Travelers"

Out of nowhere, a Michigan Trout
as big as a spaniel breaks
the black and white shawl
of water in front of me;

I glance at the source and in
that blurred moment I could see
wings threshing through the air
or paddles boiling through waves;

In that second, some seventeen pounds
of fish sleek and silent as stone
scoops and smacks the surface
with thunderous conviction.

Greg says "They come in from Lake
Michigan. They might stay or group up.
When the ice goes out, they come in.
This is their range. They're territorial."

Trout drifting to rest somewhere
arfing and squalling like sand coyotes,
their unruly occupancy within this clear
expanse a precise activity,

resting only til the half-light of dawn
triggers something close to fever
and they 're moving again
within a clear apron of water

I look over the bay, waiting for
a resurfacing; a steady prayer
between wave and rock follows
what agile patterns I claim as my own.

Every five years, I move
towards a territory of which I belong.
Every five years everything changes
but that I am moving. A migration built

into the blood, I scuttle towards a source
that left a mark on my soul's geography
part clock, part compass, part feral force
I drift to rest somewhere beyond

the rigmarole, the daily treading of water
holding my head above any turbulent wave
In my returning or in my remaining,
It is a long, hard swim either way.

Doing Time

Like Icktome you wander
the indifferent darkness
within the maximum security prison;
orphaned and alone, your nights have
become a narrow ache of nightmares
the kind you seldom confess.

Five years ago: the accident,
the terrible rolling and rolling,
the bodies pushed so far from
the front seat they are lifted
one by one from the trunk of that
car like white rabbits of hideous
magic, their fur dull with terror,
horror in their pale pink eyes;

and how your own brown skin
fell away in intensive care, regret
seized its claws in you, clung to you
and shook you like some bizarre
ragdoll or some diamondback
rattler, dusty and warm
you, too, just want to be left
alone and you pray this hard until
even your wounds, raw and open,
are glistening with tears.

I heard it too; that hollowing sound
of the immutable; the grieving song

you would lift to your lips each day
and at night try to drink away
the sight of bodies
weightless and ragged,
like Jesus in the sky
they tilt and loom towards you

in the house in which you live,
where even in darkness
I do not travel,
where the door is thick and heavy
and I could never kick it down.

Still Born

Pearl-white, we bathed you,
cocooned in soft flannel folds,
and delivered you like an effigy
to the nurse, her head shook once as
she touched your chest, your starfish hands,
your tiny head, elongated and wet with anguish.

The coolant in the room begins to hiss
(you would've shivered and cried for home—
there, a bassinet, gauzed in ivory lace
and a rocking chair wait, heaping with gifts,
one, a t-shirt that reads, "Spoiled Rotten—)

But, what did it feel like, the burden
of mottled birth unto cold, wet, sheets?
Ghost-like and timid, what did you feel?
The paralysis of silence, cold steel
against your spine, your body caging
tiny murmurs of warmth, a stubborn secret?

As the spasms boil within an amniotic river,
a gray-green meconium swaddles you
your tiny neck, swollen and collared,
drops the weight gladly into gloved hands
reluctance is your only grace
your birth, an empty, still relief.

Your sparrow-heart collapsed in dark ponds
of blood; Lovely pearl, did you feel her

legs quiver around you, their hands struggle
to resurrect you? Did you hear the sputter
of the aspirator? Or the sharp ping of
the surgical knife as it hit the floor?

Would you have carried us, let us reconcile
the seconds of your life into years just once?
We would press these lips against your chest
till the heart-tones leapt across the screen
like silvery sprites— instead, a harsh, blank,
lunatic silence levels the walls around us.

See your mother now: her breasts bound
and swollen, weeping with the bluish dew
of new milk. Here body, emptied of its manifest,
morning-heavy with beginnings,
we attend a deeper birthing now
we attend a deeper birthing now.

The Origin of Envy

And now I am fifteen and
not allowed to be
knock-kneed and hair stiff
I had no reason to sit up straight
in eight hour nothing its
and I am beyond reasonable
most of the time
I hate my stepfather

For no good reason while
the nice girls confiscate
class rings and wear
their diaphragms
most of the time
I wear sunglasses
straddle the toilet
to reach the exhaust fan
smoke cigarettes to the bone
I make myself sick

wanting to be like them and then not
making no attempt to
conceal my contempt
for the cheerleaders of
stupid happiness senior high
the only time I felt

Anything made a difference
came at sixteen, no eighteen

When, among the faint girls
and football morons,
the crowd parted like the Red Sea
and I step forward to the Burners
of Bensen, the patron saint
of Mr. Harris' seventh hour
biology lab I stand before
the petri dishes and carefully rowed
exacto knives, so utterly fascinated
with the colony of fruit flies
emerging from bananas, brown & rotting
with the horse fetus floating like
a grotesque pickle in
cloudy brine of formaldehyde

Then, Mr. Harris—
the little ferret biology teacher
said I was a "show-off"
an eager first volunteer
to dissect the large black bass
to splay and scoop the long
pearl-like strands from
a rubbery cavity of flesh
Harris and his egg-white smile
saying to me: "Do you have the
stomach for this?"

I can't believe I'm my age
and still want to carve my name
into wooden banisters
to skip class to smoke
that I still desire to take that knife
into my hand and, in a dainty manner,
sink it deep below the layer of
sinewy back muscles

beyond the tiny bladder
and brackish yellow liver
to the iridescent pearls
with an expert hand so swift
and steady no one would have
the nerve to question.

My good Fortune (for Joy)

One day my son declares:
There are dogs in your future—
mixed bloods with no collars
decent, loyal, dogs of ambition
dogs with masters and dogs whose
masters are lost without them;

There will be dogs, apocalyptic and haunting
great loping animals, ablaze with fury, their eyes
pin-thin lazers in the mist, dogs
afraid of nothing.

Dogs who'll fetch bodies of water for you.
dogs who know their way in the rain
they'll wander through your past, come
when they're called

There will be dogs with thick claws
paws that dig and do so with grand ceremony,
dogs with great strands of drool
dogs who smell and whose only
desire is to smell polite company

Dogs, at the dimmest olfactory hint,
will topple small buildings
to haul ass in your direction
sidewinding and buttramming
their way towards you,

dogs who will gather at the dish
to sniff the quorum and chew the chow
lick themselves and remember fondly
of chasing deer and marking buicks
and then in, Dog Council, howl in
your honor, a '49 in dog-years
"she was that shinnobe poem maker,
and she had some dogs, way aa hey hey hey".

By the Sound Of It

— for Danielle

I think I know what sound is:
Waves of impulse inducing
sensations produced in
the organs of the ear—further
molecular aspects fail me

but little hammers tripping
against the ear drum or
tiny black eighth notes
with feet dancing in
one ear and out the other—
the pointless route our
parents suggested
all information followed—

That is sound.
That is also what sound looks like;

like tin horn gadgets, metal half moons
paraphernalia stuck in the ear to swallow sound
or your two hands cupped to catch
a minute melody or a voice overwhelmed
that too is sound when we lift up over
sounding to listen to what we can't possibly
hear—

and that is where the breaks occurs
between sound and sight and feeling
but never hearing—

Let me try this:
You have raised two sons
with the language of earth and fire
of wind and water
You have raised two sons who bake
and cool fat fists of words
they shape and knead
the raw air like dough
words that rise softly
or sharply or soothingly
I don't know this, I cannot hear
the words but I hear the soundings . . .

when at the pow wow, they signed to you
you signed back for "drum" and I hear that
one son holds a rattle and feels the soundings
tiny seed dancers in dark tunnels of horn
and one son presses hands against the wall
to lift up over sounding to feel the color
of our songs, brilliant and deafening

and when mitch walking elk sang the blues
and teased the menominee and talked about new
cages I saw those words flutter like wings
between you, a clasped hand upon an open palm
a quick brush of fingers against the heart

we lift up over sounding to feel shape and form
to hear color and texture, to even taste the
thick blue of our heavy sadness in Clapton's
"White Room"

sounds permeate recede fade
then echo again somewhere out of sight
soundings unlike words I know

the impact, the penetration is
not a bouncing off like impulses
but like a resonance within us
you know what I mean

show me with your hands
what I am long to hear
then show me with your hands
what I am trying to say.

Homing Song: Two Stanzas

                    Because any place
you affix as home is an astonishment
Destiny or destination— *you are home*
and you know instinctly how to doubt it
a talent for searching, you begin
with maps and roots and tributaries
in a backyard or in a city park
unearthing cedar systems or star charts
or at your father's cabin
mapping the riverlogic of the Nemakagan
while otters skim and pack the trail
for you, while sand coyotes pull in
midnight air, and sing a capella
all the lonely way back
to you

And you sing back, throwing out
round songs to anonymous canyons
and the fine criminal lives
you admire and while
Invoking nothing more than the
comfort of the faraway familiar,
echoes like whispers
the sound of a descending star
your own long distance
it's all the same
Once you were reminded
of the throatsingers in Canada
as a child cried behind you

Each enhanced private legends
you used to decipher alone,
tremeloes come back
signifying you, signifying them
at the same time, a song
means all of us.

Found Poem or Sometimes I Hate My Job

"What is the first sound
you hear?"

Reply from the corner. "A gunshot."

Eight grade giggle. Ho.

Walter Uses Knife. Hunkpapa Sioux.

He's ignored. Later written up.
Later suspended.

The guest author makes a point.
the daily heart, at 100,000 beats
alpha waves ten times that
the earth being water 90 percent
waves constant, lunar phases
wind patterns day in day
out hip hop
tick tock tick tock tick tock
(Homeroom teacher calls
me that.)

Guest author.
Answer is heartbeat. Arterial
sounds in utero, pre-natal lullaby,
poet in the school, I make my point.

He makes his.

Ho.

Trickster

when the sun rises, he will be there
remaining after he is asked
to leave; he does not hear this
or this: "No, you can't"
"it has never been done"
he laughs and never sleeps
and ask with a voice
like a canyon
"Will you write poems about me?"

And then suddenly he is warm emerald water
a tide coming this close to your feet
and then skittering away
a champion of concealment
an illusion of the landscape
— it has never been easy for me
a whisper that drains like ground glass
from memory,
or like a child twisting gently
from your hand,
gone before you know it.

Constellations

. . . They had to name, they had to remember, or things would not be named and remembered if they did not do it. — Carlos Fuentes

These are the new stories,
our response
to the sorrow
of light arriving
and dying
the stellar maps of
story and myth
where writers find
their way back
to beginnings
riding like black
satin horses
charging the silvery landscape.

This is to remember

Our wounded and
dead. This is to remember
the names
we've given away
or never received.
This is to love the forgotten.

To Know By Heart:
Saulte St. Marie, October 1989

(for Conrad)

I.

In Batchawana Bay, a slight womanrain
casts a pewter haze while houses disappear
in shadows of the mountainous strata
pale pink ribbons of lights glide
slowly over the horizon. Here you need no maps,

One finds the way by hearts, you say. While
Pre-cambrian shields bear the scars of our absence
stories of how Anishinabe blood shored into stones,
of how the old man returned them to soft graves
We were here. We're still here. This place.

II.

The colors are different at Blind River, you say
there, your map is the canvas, your colors
the reflection of flint upon water and ridge
your unusual recall— a palette for heartbreak.

When you run to the petroglyphs, you leave behind
the poison of frustration— like the paintings
of the bushmen, the wind whirls away scorpion patterns
above your head, beneath your heart until the heart
can rise high above any pain of history
any pain of remembering.

III.

We step into the trading post while a black dog removes
himself slowly from the entrance. He is tolerant
of the tourists and has grown sadly arthritic, this one
who could sleep for nights under a sky of ice and stars.
He belongs here and we do not.

We wander alone through aisles of mass production
of miniature canoes and other half-priced authenticities
until we fall silent at the slight of insane opulence:
a foxskin tossed amidst a display of carved pipes and katchinas
I felt stupid and shy about tears I could not show you

When you explained how the templehairs of moose are dyed
and trimmed close into the shapes of flowerbuds. Before
leaving, you hand me a gift— a small carved bear.
Makwa, my dodem rises, swelling with the warmth of wood,
and the fenugreek odor of hands carving away the difference.

"Makwa" is the Ojibwe term for "bear"; "Dodem" is loosely
translated to refer to totemic ancestor.

In September: Ode to Tomatoes

In September, the order of business
will always begin with tomatoes
the passionate fruit
of defiant grandmothers
of bachelor lords
in their kitchens of chaos
and of the occasional gardeners like myself
who can marvel the wonders of nature
while complaining of lower back pain.

Even then, the flaming Big Boys
and voluptuous Romas gather themselves
in dishpans, in aprons, yes, even at the doorstep
waiting for the enthusiasm of an early riser
to spill with poetic love
over a Mason or a Kerr of the stewed,
the brewed, the blended, the pureed:
this is destiny,
this immortality,
this is salsa
In the dead of winter!

Tomatoes suspended in jars,
smiling their fetal smiles
outshining the corn relish
and the bony heaps of mutant squash
23 PINTS OF TOMATO MARMALADE
CANNOT HELP BUT PERSIST WITH THE IDEA OF
SPRING

amidst the basement darkness
and the stacks of dying Milwaukee Journals.

Yes, even though we walk through valleys
of shadowy Death,
we will always can tomatoes
we will ladle together
the green into red
secrets into sauce
we can because we can
and not because we must.

Here in America

(for Pompeyo Lugo Mendez while at
Lac Courte Oreilles, November 1985)

Here in America, he will say,
where wheat falls endlessly
beneath the cutter's blade
where women in summer dresses
stir their rich espresso
write poetry and compare affairs,
you are not afraid of ignorance,

You are not afraid to speak plainly
or to confront. In my country
young poets sing and have pistols
forced into their mouths
by the security forces. Those who live
bear a four-inch scar
so close to carotid
that any heart stops at the sight
of its fierceness.

When he says the word "political"
the sound is like the fast click
of stiletto heels on a city street.
He looks into his hands to find the words—
how can he show what he seen?
It is a thin language, this English.

Like Neruda, he does not wish to please Them,
to sing their love songs, or to compose

clever lyrics about the homeland. He would
rather stumble forever in darkness
than pretend to marvel at the blaze
of burning buildings
or at the death of light itself.

While he sings of home, his eyes close
as if in a dream in reverence— we cannot tell.
And when he plays his guitar at daybreak
he takes us to the place
where a mother is singing in Guarani
to her infant son Pompeyo
songs to awaken the Americans
from their long and murky slumber.

Mission at White Earth

1. While we walked around the cemetery
a crane flew over, a pterodactyl
against a sky filled with thunderheads
we read each marker, matched names
with names, until we come to "Tumahdee
infant daughter of . . ." Pennyroyal
has grown thick around the gravesite
and Phillip gently pulls away
the blue medicine of our relatives
until a proper clearing is made once again.

2. Back then, Uncle Himhim tells us,
the Jesuits had a mission
here at White Earth, translating
gospels into Chippewa, routing
the children of all the villages
into their schools. At Christmas,
the children brought home memorized
verses from catechism class
and shared sacks of peppermint sticks
and cinnamon buttons with the oldtimers
slow to learn the English, he says and laughs.

3. At the Cass County Museum,
Phillip asks the volunteer behind the desk
about the bandolier bag displayed with photos
of White Earth Anishinabeeg; I point to
the glass case that holds property
of our families but she only works on Thursdays

and does not know about ownership
Phillip writes down a description of the bag
in his journal and whispers "Let's get out of here." The volunteer
seems relieved to tabulate our visit
in the museum guest book.

4. Before we leave White Earth, we return
to mission school, still
the tallest building here. Over here,
my mother points, we would butcher chickens
with Father McHenry, over there, a huge garden
she looks at the school in silence, at the boarded
windows, at the grounds grown over with neglect
Driving past the cemetery, Phillip recalls
the found grave marker of Tumahdee, my mother's brother
and it is promised, upon return, we will plant flowers

For Children Who Earn Time

Like a dangerous mural
on the walls of an underground transit
Antone dances across the gymnasium
of the correctional center
his long black hair
as though on fire
trails in its own inspired dance
his thin legs set in time
with the drum
"I used to dance fancy" he says
while the singer, an ex-offender
assesses the balance of stick against hide
the voice within the universe
grace within chaos.

The unit counselor observes
how Antone dances alone, this
common failure to engage
this low-impulse control
he makes notes on his staff chart
and calls in those
who have earned free time
Antone curses him, filing
into line with the others
they circle each other
like cautious wolves
it is a lonely round
and a dance they despise.

Within the chemdep unit
aboard a thin mattress, Antone
must dream to stay alive
he must imagine the smell
of maple syrup, the quiet conversations
over bowls of hot milk and bread
Auntie, pausing over black coffee
tries to remember how old the boy is now
they imagine each other
but cannot remember faces
since that time in Watersmeet,
when Antone danced fancy
and Auntie watched carefully
each time.

Fever Dreams

Through the open window
the trilling of crickets
like tiny clocks mark time
breaking the silence in my room.
I am weakened by an illness
I don't try to understand
I wait for the signs
I have learned to look for.
In a masquerade of fever-soaked sheets
I can hear myself talking in sleep
while my bed rises like an elevator
or like a plane shifting and wheeling
with the jet stream in my room
past piggy banks and coat hooks.

If I pay attention I can read the wattage
on the light bulb hanging dormant
from the cobwebbed ceiling
the dolls in the closet
shiver at the spectacle:
the rising and falling at will
the calliope of colors
the sight of me bouncing off
the walls and ceiling
spitting and sparking like a
distempered farm cat.

But it causes me no great concern
the drowsy laughter aboard a bed gone afloat

I've pulled up anchor and set sail
on a voyage of the sublime
like a beery-eyed sailor I call out
to my consorts in crime
the timid dollies huddle
in the closet clinging
to the Buster Browns.

It takes some convincing
but I descend to the island of sleep
later, a falling star will skid
over the tops of trees
and I will hear it
the wind will twirl sleep
like a luscious summer fan
into my eyes
the half-dressed dollies of the closet
will close their porcelain eyes
their breath coming so evenly in the darkness.

Water Poem: A Convergence

A small wood turtle staggers slowly
rocking to lift herself from the river
steadied she can still feel the pull
of the moon's blue rings; it's not
a simple act, resisting a river
both beautiful and dangerous
a river that pulls us in
with a logic of its own.

Today I stood remembering
this metaphor of persuasion
at the convergence of the
Wisconsin and the Eau Claire
I imagined the struggle: how
the body and the hardness of
reason would ride out
the blurry rebellion
toppling like twinbirds,
within a cage of bone.

Then while fishing, I waded through
weeds to retrieve Saxon's tangled line
branches lost to the thwack and swirl
of persuasive currents
float by like broken bodies
of shipwrecked suitors
I stand for a moment to regain balance
while small perch whirl around
my thighs like raw silk

and for that moment any fear
of dark water is forgotten.

The patternless weave and resistance
of this watery landscape conspires
a romance with drowning
but to stand or even swim
seems the secret to balance
between feverish shifts of twilight
that pull us in
and the rise of dark currents
that hold us in
we are at once disconnected and tethered
to this great gray mystery
while smooth stones dream of wings
beaks and gills gasp for air.

Evelyn Searching: To My Sister

Could I tell you how it is
to search the vacant faces
like lockers at a bus station,

to spend three days and two nights
waiting for the right time
to say father
or even sister?

Would it matter if I said
the looking and the finding
could split you in two
send you into empty caverns
of silence, fearful of the sound
of your own voice?

From White Earth to El Paso
the air grows thin and dry
Mexicans and Indians drift back
and forth between Juarez and El Paso
while the days dance red-hot through
the streets of old army barracks
turned neighborhoods:
This my father calls home.

My father is from Enemy Swim
where warriors baffled their enemies
by swimming the waters endlessly at night.
Here, the Rio Grande is a thin vein

transporting dust and deliverance
Here, an enemy could walk across in silence.

Sister, I stand long and far from
any punishing storm of regret
and see in you how strangers
become fathers become strangers
in time and of choice.

And still we'll return— we always do
— as daughters or as mothers
lifting our children high above our heads
to change the color of the sky.

Prayer for Women Filled With Grace

Women who go hungry
delicately drink their tears
tipping hands like
lacy teacups to their mouths
whisper "All gone"
to themselves and
to their orphaned bodies;

Women going hungry
are eating themselves
not like Grandmother Spider
drawing a web from her body
spinning threads of glass
into death's timid puzzle,

but like a wolf gnawing to
free herself from steel jaws
women who go hungry are like wolves
hiding for days in their clothing
a burrow to warm their ivory bodies
lifting themselves in sacrifice
in a cult of suffering

To those women going hungry
whose porcelain faces are feverish
with blame, whose voices mimic
the clear thin weeping of August rain:

Draw up like buckets from hollow wells!
Draw up like tin cups between prison bars!
The rich ooze of anger
will twirl around the tongue
while the eyes grow filmy with pleasure
it is this ritual of indulgence
that spoons and spills from within
the only appetite left to survive
this perfect hunger spell.

My Mother and I had a Discussion One Day

and she said I was quite fortunate
to have two sons
and I said how is that? and she said
with daughters you worry for them
birth control, childrearing,
you worry for them, the threat of rape,
and then there is the wedding expense.
I looked into her tired eyes
and clouded face and saw
that she was quite serious.
Yes, but, I said,
boys eat more.

My mother and I had a discussion one day
and she said why do they call it
women's music?
and I said because they sing it,
take from it, feel good and strong
when they walk away from it
while we sit here this is going on.
Are you telling me, my mother said
up until now, I have been listening
and no women have been singing?
and I said that is right
and she said that was ridiculous
and hummed a tune
of her own.

My mother and I had a discussion one day
and she said why do you want to leave
this house, it is a fine house?
and I said I didn't think there was much of a market
for a nosewiper, a kitchen keeper,
an under the bed sweeper
and she said my smart mouth
would get me in trouble one day
and I looked at her scarred knuckles
and quivering chin and realized
that I had spit in the face
of a thousand thousand women and I wept
with my mother.

Losing to the Breakfast of Champions

I suppose I imagine it to be much worse
than it is: the flakes that are not flaky
the toasties that don't feel toasted
the wheat that boasts of germ and bran
is closer to shrewd than shred

It is not as though I regret the ritual
of adding the sugar, the fruit
the cream, the spoon
or the mantra of each yawning deliverance
to mouth from spoon to bowl
to spoon to mouth

Perhaps it is the voice of my mother
insisting that all of this be eaten
or the newsclipping on the refrigerator
anecdotes of spoiled children
the horrid breakfasts of sweet rolls
and hot chocolate

Or the hideous claims that cold pizza
and party punch contribute to street crime
or the rumor that sheila beddingheim
grew up to be quite promiscuous
because she ate no breakfast at all.

Winter Farm Auction

The pathway to their garden
has all but disappeared
onion sets like angry fists
have pushed themselves
through the frozen soil.

Pumpkin hearts have split
themselves in two
angry at being left behind
their vines
stiff and dry as snake skin
tangle in the molding leaves.

Stalks of corn lean together
like old women
pausing to mourn the scowl
of cold November winds.

Tilted seed caps block
the afternoon sun while eyes
follow the Homelite chainsaw
black and heavy it goes for 25.

An Amish woman wears her cap recklessly
raising her number high for doilies
in a porcelain dishpan.

Somewhere a clang of horseshoes
and old garden tools are brought out

into the open like quarreling roosters
they are examined by the crowd of gamblers.

The auctioneer assembles the parcels
into a wooden crate and raises them up
high above the crowd, he asks
who will give him a dollar bill.

Grace's Funeral

It's a dying shame that it's
always an adult who wallows in
serious error with such explanations
"Like sleeping but then it's not."
Children, emotional spot checkers
at funerals tug and pull for answers
asking the forgivable questions
wondering whether Grace can fly now.

At Auntie's house, the relatives
sit with plates of food on their laps
with plastic forks and no appetite
But the children are indeed hungry
for stories of the Dead People:
the neighbor who mistook his wife
for an outlaw and shot her
a simple case of mistaken identity.
This happens.

Or the boy who watched his twin brother
choke on a chickenbone and only the day before
had asked an adult about the heimlich manoeuvre
or the aunt who never married but would often
sleepwalk and once off a bridge she fell
into the shallows holding the morning mail
most everyone certain she could not fly.

Club Med at UxMal, Yucatan

The water in the toilet is drinkable
the tap water is not, I am warned
the paradoxes get less amusing as
we stroll through the makeshift mercado
on the grounds before UxMal
the children of Mayan traders sit
playing with sticks and stones
while guatemalan trinkets
and toys are sold dirt cheap as we say. Uncleanliness,

a disease of despair, is a problem
mothers must battle in a country
where sanitized water is confined
to drinking only from crystal in
the dining rooms of only the
finest restaurants—
a simple washing
of hands is a luxury not allowed

It is by force of habit then
that I allow myself to break
away from the group and entice
a young mother to take
a break and sit
with me at the refreshment stand—

She is about sixteen and saddled with
an infant and a two-year-old,
the baby wrapped with a shawl

46

close to her small adolescent body
the toddler, brown, thin, and docile,
clings to her side
to me they all look like children—
and so I offer a wet cloth
and motion to the child, using

a clumsy language to indicate "wash"
and she does, delicately cleaning
the dust from the chin and eyelids
of her baby. She grins and
looks softly at me and then away
my Mayan worse than my Spanish,
I smile too, looking toward UxMal,
missing my own children, feeling
cool and unclean.

Veteran's Dance, 1995

— after Oklahoma City

During this round
I wanted to think of you
then, when each step
meant something
and you would
be out of
the mirrored building
and in front
of me
dancing too,

instead I danced alone
under the stars
and the wild sadness
of Oklahoma City
spoors of light
burnish
the newborn darkness
there is a blank moon
tonight,

and no one to sing to.
This is the worst war
we've ever seen:
surrounded and unarmed,
shadows
unravelling everywhere.

Insomniac

We say "wake up, I can't sleep:"
but that's only half true

We want the world to know
we are stumbling around in the dark

standing on one foot, staring out windows
flipping channels, starting jigsaw puzzles

We'd like you to know that
but, please, don't wake up

they dynamics get scrambled
and it won't work then

then it's table for two,
double-dare conversation, courtesy

Rather we'd be left to languish
in the living alone, like little

girl dress-up, clopping around
in unlaced cognition, socking pillows

despising the Sleepers, listening
for little chokes of air

coming from the serene dark
here, we left to our own devices

Toe-puppets as consorts, we slay you
on the twilight stage. Rest deeply

in the knowing we toss and spin
and backflip on the trampoline

of adrenalin while you sleep sweetly
lids flutter, muscles jerk and twitch

while we pace and pace and you rest in peace
your sleep sounds a soporific vanishing point.

The 500-year-old Poem

—*"Come on, brothers and sisters. Let's go home."*
— Frank Montano, Anishinabe, Red Cliff

This poem began five hundred years ago
this morning when I traced the numbers
of generations of our grandchildren,
Mr. Columbus. The great-great-great-greats
of offspring that discovered you
on that caribbean island
you claimed for your
European benefactors—
they are here today, we are still here
on that island, on other islands
we are still here on the deltas
to the South, rebuilding our
traditional. shelters after hurricanes,

we are still here, gathered around
the great lakes, giving thanks for
the good grain, manomin, and planning
our harvest ceremonies, while our
grandmothers and grandfathers
teach us the real old songs
of gratitude and of reverence. We are still

here in the Black Hills and at Big Mountain
and at James Bay, where big business and
big government tries to rid itself of
the nuisance of native people— we are here
in solidarity at the fencelines in Hopi

and Navajoland, at the boatlandings in
Balsam Lake and in Solun Springs, and in
Lac du Flambeau— indeed, we are even at
the mouth of the Mississippi, where the
drum carries a true thanksgiving prayer
for the land and the water that holds and
carries our healing medicines. We are here
at Kahnawake and Kahnasatake,
and at Akwesasne where our spiritual leaders
in their own language say, "No more"
to the harassment, to the removal,
to the imprisonment, and to what they say in
America, "Development" because they know what
they know, and they are praying
as hard as they can that you will come
to know it as well. We are here, we are still

here, on clouded land at White Earth, where
Anishinaabe Akeeng and women warriors like
Winona LaDuke say,

"500 years of taking is
long enough," say,

"We *can* return to the
last of our original lands, say,

"The U.S. Government has failed
to uphold the spirit
and the letter of the law of the land
according to the Treaty of 1837, 1854
and 1872 . . .
and we are going
to recover these stolen lands,
acre by acre,

inch by inch,
even if we have to buy them back."
That is what she said, and that
is what I say.

We are here. We are still here

beyond any borders that might be construed
between our sisters and brothers of South
and Central America, where the children
of Rigoberta Menchu teach one another
how to read and write— tracing with sticks
indigenous words into the ground, so they
do not forget how to speak to their elders
so they do not forget, that they, too are
Indigenous. I tell you this, Mr. Columbus:
we are recreating the enemy's language
as the Creek poet says into words of
resistance, into words of affirmation,
into words that help us to fully understand
the stronghold of colonialism exists
first in the mind. Somewhere in
Guatemala, a child can still pray
in a language born out of struggle
and into survival. Somewhere in the Yucatan
the people now whisper, "We are here, We are
still here."

So to the generations of offspring born in 1492
I give you this: a poem that has taken
500 years to write. It has taken some
time to find the words,
to trace their beginnings
It takes time to recall the stories
It takes time to remember and recover

the strength and pride
in our sovereignty
to say what we have to say
but believe this: Waiting is
worth it, the oldtimers tell us.
Time is seamless, without a beginning
or end. Mr. Columbus, Today marks no
greater discovery than our ability
to survive, our ability to speak for
ourselves, and our patience with
those who followed you
to this place, and into our homes. What
better way to celebrate a good day within
another harvest season: We are here
We are still here. We are where we belong.

Denise Sweet is an Anishinaabe enrolled at White Earth, and a professor of Humanistic Studies at UW-Green Bay where she also serves as chair for the American Indian Studies program. She teaches creative writing, literature and mythology, and a travel seminar that involves fieldwork among the indigenous people of the Yucatan Peninsula and Guatemala. She has served as a poet-in-residence in public and tribal schools as well as at the Grand Marais Art Colony and the Apostle Islands National Lakeshore.

Her poetry has appeared in *Sustaining the Forest, The People, and the Spirit, Calyx, Sinister Wisdom, Akwekon, Another Chicago Magazine, Returning the Gift, Women Brave In the Face of Danger* and others. *Days of Obsidian, Days of Grace: Four Native American Writers* (Poetry Harbor) devotes a section to her work. Her work has also been commissioned by the Great Lakes Inter-tribal Council, and has been featured in gallery exhibits to include a 2nd place recognition at the Sante Fe Indian Market in 1995.

Sweet currently lives on the Wisconsin Oneida reservation with her partner, Charlie Hornett. She is the mother of two fine Anishinaabe sons, Damon (22) and Vaughn (20).

First Book Awards For Poetry

Established in 1992 in conjunction with the Returning The Gift Festival, The North American Native Authors Poetry Award is given for a first book by a Native writer. Named the Diane Decorah Award in memory of a Native writer and supporter of other Native authors, its winners published by The Greenview Review Press are:

1992   Gloria Bird *Full Moon On The Reservation*

1993   Kimberly Blaeser *Trailing You*

1994   Tiffany Midge *Outlaws, Renegades and Saints*

1995   Denise Sweet *Songs For Discharming*

1996   Charles G. Ballard *Winter Count Poems*

1997   Deborah A. Miranda *Indian Cartography*